EXETER

A shortish guide

Robert Hesketh

Bossiney Books · Launceston

First published 2009 by Bossiney Books Ltd
Langore, Launceston, Cornwall PL15 8LD
www.bossineybooks.com
ISBN 978-1-906474-10-2
Printed in Great Britain by R Booth Ltd, Penryn, Cornwall

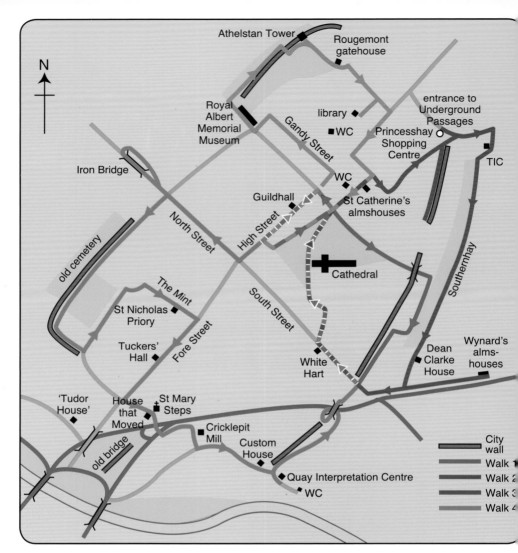

A sketch map showing the four walks which explore the city centre. A fifth walk (see page 24) covers the Quay area and a sixth covers the port of Topsham (see page 28)

Acknowledgements
The maps are by Nick Hawken.
The cover is based on a design by Heards Design Partnership.
All photographs are by the author or from the publishers' own collection.
The photograph of Cricklepit Mill was taken by kind
permission of Devon Wildlife Trust.

Introduction

Exeter is one of England's most rewarding cities to get to know. Every major stage of its long and fascinating history, over 2000 years of continuous settlement, can be traced on the ground. Most of the city's great legacy of visible history lies within the tight 38 hectare compass of its ancient walls, making it ideal for exploration on foot.

This book is therefore divided into five short walks with sketch maps and photographs, which include all Exeter's major sites and much more besides. A sixth walk explores Topsham, its ancient quay and streets of Stuart and Georgian houses. Each walk could be completed in an hour, but there is so much to see that half a day is a better allowance.

Despite several violent attacks and sieges down the centuries, including sacking by Vikings in 1003 and the devastating Blitz of 1942, Exeter retains a wealth of historic buildings. The Cathedral with its two Norman towers and richly decorated west front is outstanding; so is the beautiful Close, a circuit of historic buildings.

The medieval Guildhall is the oldest municipal building still in regular use in England. Rougemont Castle, Tuckers' Hall, St Nicholas Priory, the Underground Passages and medieval Exe Bridge are also key historic sites open to visitors.

Exeter's attractive Quay, a ring of red stone churches and a range of timber-framed houses (including one saved from development and moved to its present site on wheels) offer further scope for exploration along streets which follow the patterns laid by Britons, Romans and Saxons, crossing and re-crossing the city walls. Nearly three quarters of these walls still stand, a 2.5 km circuit including long sections founded on durable Roman masonry.

Some other books about Exeter

Cherry, Bridget and Pevsner, Nikolaus, *Devon*, The Buildings of England series, Yale University Press, 2004 (formerly Penguin)

Harvey, Hazel, *Exeter Past*, Phillimore, Chichester, 1996

Hoskins, W G, *Devon*, Phillimore, Chichester, 2003 and Collins, 1954

Hoskins, W G, *Two Thousand Years in Exeter*, Phillimore, Chichester, 1960, 1963 and 2004

Williams, Geoff, *An Absurdly Short History of Exeter*, Bossiney Books, Launceston, 2008

Timeline

National events	Exeter events	Exeter sites
Iron Age c700BC-AD50	Isca (Exeter) established	Quay, Walk 5 Bartholomew St, Walk 4
Roman occupation AD50-c410	Legionary fortress, bath house and forum built. Topsham a port	City walls, Walks 1-4
Anglo-Saxon settlement and later Viking raids	Abbey founded c670. Attacks and sieges, Exeter sacked 1003	City walls, Walks 1-4
Norman Conquest, 1068-9	Western Rebellion William besieged Exeter	Rougemont Castle, Walk 3
Norman church building	New Norman cathedral begun 1112	Cathedral, Walk 1 St Nicholas Priory, Walk 4
Trade increases by land and sea	First stone bridge over Exe. Topsham rivals Exeter as a port	Exe Bridge, Topsham Quay, Walks 5 & 6
Wool becomes the foundation of England's wealth	Exe Island reclaimed. Leats cut, mills built	Cricklepit Mill, Tuckers' Hall, Walks 4 & 5
Black Death kills half population but England recovers during C15	Guildhall rebuilt 1468. Wool trade revived. Central churches rebuilt. Secular building	Guildhall, White Hart, Wynards, Walks 1 and 2
Henry VIII declares himself Head of C of E. Dissolution of the monasteries	St Nicholas and Polsloe priories dissolved. Exeter besieged by Prayer Book rebels	St Nicholas Priory, Walk 5
English Civil War 1642-8. Royalist forces eventually defeated by Parliament	Exeter besieged by Royalist then by Parliamentary armies. Princess Henrietta born Exeter 1644	City walls, Walks 1-4. Guildhall Walks 1, 3 & 4
Economy recovers from ravages of war	Custom House built. Canal widened. Major building in Topsham	Topsham, Walk 6 Quay, Walk 5

Richard Hooker, 1554-1600, was an Exeter theologian who – unusually for his time – stressed tolerance and inclusiveness. His statue can be found in the Cathedral Close

Monmouth Rebellion 1685	Judge Jeffreys tries local rebels in Guildhall	Guildhall, Walks 1, 3 & 4
William of Orange 'accepts' English crown	William enters Exeter in triumph, 1688	West Gate, Walk 4
Improved road transport late C18 & early C19. Coaching era	Exeter develops as a coaching centre with fine inns and England's first 'hotel' and Georgian crescents	Royal Clarence, Turk's Head Inn, North Road Bridge, Walks 1-5
Industrial Revolution fosters economic and population growth	New warehouses at Quay. Suburbs expand. Railway arrives 1844, extends rapidly	Quay, Walk 5 Royal Albert Museum, Walk 3
Expansion of education	University established 1922	Phoenix Arts, Walk 3
World War 2 1939-45	Exeter blitzed 1942	Memorial ruins, Walk 2
Post-war reconstruction. Major road-building, motor car age	Large areas of city completely redesigned. New roads and bridges built	Princesshay, Exe Bridges, Walks 2 & 5

The river crossing was the key to the original site of the city. This is the surviving part of the medieval Exe bridge, built about 1200

An outline of the city's history

Exeter was already an established settlement with a quay and overseas trade when the Romans built a legionary fortress there and made Topsham their outport about AD 50. Around AD 120-30 Exeter was redeveloped and became the regional capital, with walled defences.

The Roman armies had withdrawn from Britain by 410. After a series of battles, Exeter came under the control of Saxon Wessex. The Abbey was founded in 670. Viking armies attacked in 851, 876, 893 and 1001, sacking the city in 1003.

In 1068-9 Exeter was besieged by King William I, who built Rougemont Castle after the city surrendered. Work on the Norman cathedral

The riverside areas of Exeter have been developed in recent times in a deliberately 'Mediterranean' manner, and on sunny days are very popular with locals and visitors alike

began in 1112, but the rest is gothic and was completed in 1370.

Exeter's wealth was founded on wool. Leats were cut and mills built by the Exe. Domestic and export trade grew. As the strategic and economic centre of the West, Exeter was besieged by Perkin Warbeck in 1497 and by the Prayer Book rebels in 1549. Initially held for Parliament in the Civil War, it was taken by Royalists in 1643, but retaken by Parliament in 1646 – the last siege of its history.

Trade recovered after the war and Exeter reached the height of its wool-based prosperity.

Topsham was rebuilt. Although Devon's wool industry later declined, Exeter grew, first as a coaching centre with many inns and then, from1844, as a railway hub.

Blitzed in 1942, Exeter was substantially redesigned and rebuilt after 1945. New roads and shopping precincts contrast sharply with the city's surviving historic buildings. These span every age from the Romans onward, but Exeter is a lively bustling place, by no means just a museum.

Top right: Rougemont Castle

Below right: The doorway of number 11, Cathedral Close, formerly the residence of the Archdeacon of Barnstaple, a medieval house modified in the seventeenth century

The Cathedral

Built on the site of the Roman camp established by the Second Augustan Legion, Exeter Cathedral has a long history. Around 670 a Benedictine monastery with a minster church was established and St Boniface, the patron saint of Germany, was educated here. The minster church became a cathedral in 1050 when Leofric, Bishop of Crediton and St Germans (Cornwall), moved his see to Exeter.

In 1114 a new cathedral in the Norman style was begun. The present building retains the two massive transeptal towers of the Norman cathedral, which still dominate the city's skyline. However, the main body of the cathedral seen today is the one John Grandisson, bishop from 1327 to 1369, saw part finished, but found 'marvellous in beauty', predicting it would 'surpass every gothic church in England and France.'

Completed some years after Grandisson's death, the new cathedral fulfilled his hopes. Like the earlier Norman cathedral, it took nearly a century's work. Its last major addition and crowning glory was the great image screen on the west front. Richly sculpted, it provides a most impressive entrance. Originally, it was painted.

Even more striking is the magnificent ribbed vaulting of the roof. Stretching 90 m (300 ft) from west to east and supported by the Norman towers combined with blue grey columns of Purbeck marble and ingenious external buttressing, it is the longest run of gothic vaulting in the world. This great vault lends remarkable stylistic consistency to the whole building – rivalled in England only by Salisbury Cathedral.

Lit by many windows, notably the great rose window of the west front and the equally magnificent east window with its medieval stained glass, the stone in Exeter Cathedral, much of it creamy white limestone from Beer in East Devon, has a warmth that makes it especially attractive and renders its internal decoration and furnishing so beautiful. There is much more to see than space to describe it here, but special mention must go to the richly carved pulpitum screen (1324) with its series of 17th century paintings. Above it stands the magnificent 17th century organ case.

Thomas of Witney carved the pulpitum screen and also the bishop's throne – at 23 m high the largest piece of ecclesiastical furniture in Britain. The minstrels' gallery with its fourteen carved angels, each playing a musical instrument, and the many carved and painted ceiling bosses are also great pieces of craftsmanship, best appreciated with binoculars. Under the seats of the choir stalls are a fascinating group of 13th century carved misericords. Showing a variety of people and animals (some real and some mythical), they are the oldest in England.

The astronomical clock dates from 1484, though its parts date from various centuries. It shows the earth as a golden orb at the centre of a pre-Copernican universe. Around it revolves the moon, a silver/black orb and the sun, represented by the fleur de lys.

Among many extra areas of interest is the Cathedral Library, where the *Exeter Book*, a unique collection of Anglo-Saxon poetry, is housed as well as the *Exon Domesday* of 1086.

The Cathedral Close with its peaceful grass makes an obvious centre for the city. The Cathedral also holds special events, including art exhibitions and concerts

The starting point for Walks 1 to 4 is this corner of the Cathedral Close, outside the Royal Clarence Hotel

Walk 1 The heart of the City

This short walk contains the essence of historic Exeter, with the Cathedral, Close, city wall and Guildhall. It could be completed in well under an hour, but deserves much longer.

Start with your back to the Royal Clarence Hotel in the Cathedral Close. Established in 1770 as England's first hotel, it became the Royal Clarence in 1827 when patronised by the Duchess of Clarence. Its new corporate name is The Abode Exeter. With the cathedral on your right, walk past a series of beautiful buildings on your left. Although medieval in origin, they have later additions and façades, but make a harmonious group.

Number 1, formerly Mol's Coffee House, has a flamboyant Dutch gable and bears Elizabeth I's Coat of Arms and the date 1596. This is really a Victorian façade, but the house retains genuine 16th century features inside.

The front of Number 5 dates from 1700, Number 6 from 1770. Numbers 7, 8 and 9a were originally medieval courtyard houses. Numbers 10 and 11 were once the Archdeacon of Barnstaple's residence. The front was remodelled in the 17th century in local red Heavitree stone. A splendid arched entrance surrounds a studded and carved door (photograph on page 7) similar to the Guildhall's. Numbers 12 and 13 were the Abbot of Buckfast's house, but were badly damaged in the 1942 Blitz. The surviving wing to the Close formed the gatehouse.

Continue under an iron footbridge dated 1814 and spanning a breach in the city wall. Turn right into Southernhay, containing the

most extensive Georgian terraces in Exeter. Now the haunt of solicitors and estate agents, Southernhay was designed by local builder Matthew Nosworthy in 1789.

Turn right at the footpath/cyclepath sign EXE BRIDGE and then left along the city wall. First built around AD 200, three quarters of the 2.5km long wall still stands. It has served the city well through many attacks and sieges, from the Saxon invasions and Viking raids, through medieval rebellions to the Civil War of 1642-46. Enclosing 38 hectares, the wall still defines the perimeter of central Exeter. The Guildhall, Cathedral and main shops all come within its compass and High Street, Fore Street, South Street and North Street meet at the centre ('carfax') of the walled city exactly as the Romans planned it.

Turn right into South Street, past the site of the South Gate. One of four gates guarding the old walled city, South Gate was the last to be demolished in 1819 to make way for increased traffic. Its destruction must have delighted the debtors imprisoned in the upper room. This was known as 'the shoe' as prisoners begged for alms by lowering a shoe on a string to passers by – reputedly the origin of 'living on a shoestring'.

Continue past the White Hart, a 15th century building behind a handsome Georgian façade. The high entrance arch was built to allow coaches easy access to the stables behind at a time when Exeter was the

Top left: This iron bridge spans a break in the city wall

Below left: The city wall behind Southernhay. What we see is a wall which has been repaired and upgraded many times, but the dressed purple stones of local volcanic trap are distinctive and often Roman. They are mixed in with red Heavitree sandstone, used extensively from the fourteenth century, and later brick

hub of Devon's burgeoning coach traffic. A cobbled floor leads to the yard and the older part of the inn. This includes a good 16th century parlour with moulded beams, a richly carved ceiling and fireplace.

Turn right into PALACE GATE, signed CATHEDRAL. Walk past the gatehouse, one of the better medieval survivals of the Bishop's Palace, along with the subdivided 13th century Great Hall. What the public can see of the Bishop's Palace today from the street is mainly the 1845 rebuilding, further tempered by modernisation in 1948.

Continue to the West Front of the Cathedral. To add the medieval Guildhall to your walk, return to the Royal Clarence. Turn left into MARTIN'S LANE. Walk past the Ship, a jettied Elizabethan house (see page 19) to the High Street and turn left.

Next door to the Guildhall is the 17th century Turk's Head. Here, Charles Dickens met the somnolent servant who became the model for the Fat Boy in *Pickwick Papers*. Continue down the High Street and turn first left into Broadgate and the Cathedral Yard.

The Guildhall

The earliest reference to Exeter's Guildhall was in 1160, making it one of England's oldest municipal buildings still used for meetings (at which times it is closed). Its massive pillared porch in granite and Beer stone was built in 1593 for £4 10s, but repaired and strengthened many times. The carved Doric door is also late Elizabethan and makes entrance to the huge hall, with its high collar-braced timber roof (1470), even more impressive.

The panelled walls are lined with the names of past Exeter dignitaries. Above are large portraits, including those of Princess Henrietta, daughter of Charles I, who was born in Exeter in 1644, while it was still Royalist. Beside her is General Monck, a Devonian and chief architect in the Restoration of Charles II in 1660.

The upper floor (view by special appointment) houses the city's silver and mayorial regalia. Exeter's cap and sword of maintenance, awarded by a grateful Henry VII for the city's successful stand against the Pretender Perkin Warbeck in 1497, are also on display.

Southernhay's elegant brick terraces were designed by Devon architect Matthew Nosworthy in 1789

Walk 2 The eastern quarter – Princesshay and Southernhay

Facing the Royal Clarence turn right into CATHERINE STREET and continue past the ruins of St Catherine's Almshouses (see page 18).

Turn right, signed SOUTHERNHAY QUARTER PRINCESSHAY SQUARE. Only 50m ahead turn left, signed EXETER'S UNDERGROUND PASSAGES.

The present Princesshay Shopping Centre – notable for the view of the Cathedral from Princesshay Square – was completed in 2007, replacing earlier post-war developments. These in turn had taken the place of the part of central Exeter most severely damaged during the Blitz, which devastated 15 hectares of the city centre. Forty German aircraft dropped 160 explosive bombs and 10,000 incendiaries on May 4, 1942. This one raid, by far the worst, claimed 156 lives and destroyed 400 shops and 1500 houses.

Walk ahead through the shopping precinct to another section of the city wall, which may be followed to the right for 150m to the site of the Georgian Bedford Circus and earlier Dominican Priory, before retracing your steps. Continue ahead EXETER'S UNDERGROUND PASSAGES. Turn left EXETER'S UNDERGROUND PASSAGES. The entrance (easily missed) is only 20m further ahead.

Retrace your steps 20m. Continue ahead, SOUTHERNHAY QUARTER. Take the next turning right SOUTHERNHAY EAST. Turn right in front of the Visitor Information Centre and left into Southernhay. Stroll through Southernhay's Veitch Heritage Garden, which commemorates the local Veitch family of plant hunters, collectors and nurserymen.

The large brick building at the far end of the gardens is Dean Clarke House, formerly the Royal Devon and Exeter Hospital (1741-1974). It was founded by Dr Alured Clarke, Dean of Exeter in 1741.

At the foot of Southernhay, you may want to make a diversion by turning left along busy Magdalen Steet for 100m to see Wynard's Almshouses. These Grade II* listed buildings date from 1435, when they were founded by William Wynard, the Exeter Recorder. Retrace your steps to the foot of Southernhay and continue ahead.

Otherwise, turn right from Southernhay and take the next turning right into SOUTH STREET.

Either, if you wish to join Walk Five at this point, cross the road junction and then the footbridge over the road ahead. Follow the steps down at the far side – not into the car park's turret. Turn right at street level, pass under the footbridge, and then turn right downhill with the city wall on your right. Turn left for the Quay House Visitor Centre.

Or, to return to the Royal Clarence, follow the route described more fully in Walk 1. Pass the White Hart, turn right into PALACE GATE. Continue past the West Front of the Cathedral to the start.

The Underground Passages

Exeter's medieval underground passages are unique in being open to the public. A visit begins with an introductory film, continues with a fascinating guided tour and concludes with the museum. This includes models which show how the siphon-driven system worked, tableaux explaining Exeter's archaeology and the history of its water supply, plus a selection of underground finds from the Roman through to the modern levels.

The first passages were built for the cathedral between 1347 and 1349 to carry water in lead pipes from wells beyond the city walls. The city of Exeter followed suit, building its first underground passages in 1492. Using the cut-and-cover method, with stone-lined and vaulted passages, the system was extended and deepened down to the 19th century and the beginning of modern water supplies to meet Exeter's greatly increased needs.

Blocked during the Civil War siege to prevent an underground attack, the passages found a new use during the 1942 Blitz as a bomb shelter. Some 80% of the passages survive.

Walk 3 The northern quarter including the Castle

Facing the Royal Clarence Hotel (page 10), turn left and leave the Cathedral Close by turning right through Broadgate. The Broadgate itself was demolished in 1825, at the time Tinley's stucco café was built. On the opposite corner is the imposing City Bank of 1875.

Turn right into High Street to pass the Guildhall (page 13) and the Turk's Head. Despite the 1942 Blitz and post-1945 redevelopment (sometimes said to have been even more destructive), High Street retains some fine Tudor and Stuart timber-framed buildings – best seen by looking above modern shop fronts. Some of the old houses are narrow, showing the original medieval 'burgage plots' on which they were built. Number 223/225, the most splendid of the group, has five jettied storeys and carved details.

Just beyond this building, turn left into GANDY STREET. J K Rowling, an Exeter University graduate, is said to have based Diagon Alley in her Harry Potter stories on this narrow lane. Although it mainly consists of early 19th century buildings, the line of Gandy Street is Saxon, one of several grid-plan streets from that period, including Martin's Lane and Catherine Street.

The Phoenix Arts Centre (1983), on the right at the far end, was built in 1911 as part of the University College of the South West, which became the University of Exeter in 1955, centred on its present campus towards the northern edge of the city. The Phoenix presents a varied programme, including plays, poetry, music and the visual arts.

Gandy Street makes a left turn and then leads to Queen Street. Make a short diversion left to see the dignified neo-classical entrance to the Higher Market (1834), before retracing your steps past the foot of Gandy Street to the Royal Albert Memorial Museum (RAMM).

The Museum is a solid stone Victorian gothic building completed in 1869. When it reopens in 2010 after major refurbishment it will again give a first class introduction to Exeter's history. Meanwhile, part of the city's collections are housed at the Central Library, included later in this walk. RAMM's Roman section and the preserved details from Exeter's medieval buildings are especially good. The museum has many other displays, including extensive ethnographic and natural history exhibits from around the world.

Continue along Queen Street and turn right up the slope into Northernhay Gardens. Like Southernhay (page 14), Northernhay was

Rougemont Castle

The photograph shows its early Norman gatehouse keep.

Exeter was the focus of the Western Rebellion in 1068, and was besieged by William I.

After the city surrendered (on favourable terms), the king ordered Rougemont to be built on central Exeter's highest vantage point.

He also ordered a series of similar castles to be built around Devon to quell any further unrest.

laid out in the 17th century and fortified during the Civil War, but the statues of local worthies and the huge war memorial are 19th and 20th century. The large, grim building in front is Exeter Prison, once the venue for public executions which drew large crowds.

Along the southern edge of the gardens is a particularly good section of the city wall. A narrow gate through the wall opposite the war memorial leads into Rougemont Gardens, rich with flowers in spring. Turn left onto the wall walk and follow the signs up to ATHELSTAN'S TOWER. Having seen the view, follow the lower path (the upper one is a cul de sac) above the castle's dry moat to the well preserved early Norman gatehouse keep.

Before the nearby Law Courts were built in classical style in 1774, Rougemont Castle was used for trials. The gatehouse bears a plaque to the four 'Devon Witches', women who had the grisly distinction of being the last people executed for witchcraft in England in 1682 and 1685. (Whether the 1685 execution actually occurred is disputed by some historians.)

Opposite the gatehouse is Rougemont House. First built by John Patch, a local surgeon, in 1769, it was largely remodelled in Regency style, and bears a plaque describing its history.

Turn right and walk down Castle Street. Take the first right to visit the Central Library, which acts as the Museum's city centre home until work on the Queen Street RAMM site is completed in 2010. Retrace your steps to Castle Street. Take the next turning right into High Street. Continue to a striking 6m high sculpture, The Exeter Riddle (2005). On each side of the stainless steel fins is a riddle in modern English taken from the 10th century *Exeter Book*, a treasure of Anglo-Saxon literature kept in the Cathedral Library, which contains poems such as *The Seafarer*, *The Ruin* and *The Wanderer*, as well as the epic *Beowulf*. Having racked your brains, look for the answers in the sculpture's polished spheres.

Turn left at the Riddle and after 40m turn right, signed CATHEDRAL QUARTER CATHERINE SQUARE to visit St Catherine's Almshouses. After the 1942 Blitz, which gutted a large area of central Exeter, these almshouses – originally built in 1458 by Canon John Stevens to accommodate thirteen poor men – were preserved as a memorial.

Recent archaeological excavations revealed beneath the almshouses a Roman town house with three or possibly four rooms and mosaic floors. Remains of a first century Roman fortress were also found on the site. Having seen the almshouses, walk ahead to the start.

St Catherine's Almshouses

The Iron Bridge, constructed in 1834, enabled Exeter's rapidly growing coach traffic to sail over the steep slope below

Walk 4 The western and southern quarters

Facing the Royal Clarence, turn right and almost immediately left into MARTIN'S LANE. Walk past the Ship Inn. Purportedly Elizabethan and certainly old, it was recorded during the Civil War, when the Royalist Captain Benet billeted his troops here during General Fairfax's siege.

Turn left into HIGH STREET. Only 50 m ahead on the right is Goldsmith Street, so named because medieval artisans usually grouped together and consequently streets were named after them.

Continue past the Guildhall (page 13). Just beyond the entrance to the Guildhall Shopping Centre is Parliament Street. Nicknamed 'Squeezebelly' it is the narrowest street in Exeter (the plaque claims narrowest in the world), ranging from 62 cm (25 inches) to a liberal 112 cm (45 inches). Opposite Parliament Street is the City Bank. A plaque explains the history of Exeter banking in brief.

Take the next turning right, NORTH STREET. On the right is Waterbeer Street. Another trade name, it was derived from the water bearers, who performed a vital function before piped water was readily available throughout Exeter.

Cross Paul Street and continue ahead down LOWER NORTH STREET. This leads steeply downhill to the right of the bridge. It was the northern route out of Exeter, passing by the North Gate (one of the city's four medieval gates) until that was demolished in 1769. Cross under the iron bridge. After seeing the bridge from below, return to Paul Street by climbing the steps and following the New North Road, which gives a bird's eye view of the Georgian houses in the street below.

Turn right CITY WALL WALK into BARTHOLOMEW STREET EAST. The building on the right was once a maltings, later a pottery – hence the

19

St Michael's, Mount Dinham, a Victorian church which dominates the view from above the Catacombs

bottle kiln. Keep the iron railing on your right and turn right through an iron gate when the road curves left. You are now standing above the Catacombs. These magnificent and curious tombs were built in 1837 by a private speculator who lost heavily on the venture. Fifteen people were interred here, the last in 1883, their coffins being lowered from street level into the vaults below.

For a better view of the Catacombs, follow the path down into the old graveyard. Retrace your steps to the iron gate. Turn right and follow the pavement ahead. There is a good view of Mount Dinham with its 67 m tall church spire on your right. Away beyond Exwick there are rolling green hills – Exeter is a small city and the countryside is never very far away.

The square on your left is Bartholomew's Yard. Established as a graveyard in 1636 when space in Cathedral Yard was exhausted, it was formerly rack fields for drying the woollen cloth that made Exeter rich. Three lanes in Exeter derive their names from these rack fields: Rack Street, Rackfield Place and Rackclose Lane (see below).

Follow BARTHOLOMEW TERRACE ahead and then left. Lined with attractive early 19th century houses, it stands above a well preserved section of the city wall. Arriving at the Old Chapel, take a diversion sharp right if you want to see the wall's masonry.

Retrace your steps to the Old Chapel. Turn left, ST NICHOLAS PRIORY. Take the second turning right into THE MINT, site of a mint established in 1696, the second most productive provincial mint in England. This is also the site of St Nicholas Priory.

Turn right down FORE STREET. On the right, 100 m ahead, is Tuckers' Hall – see page 22 for a description.

The entrance to The Mint, an old and narrow street which leads to St Nicholas Priory

St Nicholas Priory

This was first dedicated as a Benedictine priory in 1087. In the 12th and 13th centuries new monastic buildings were added as the priory was given gifts of land and property. Until Henry VIII dissolved England's smaller monasteries in 1536, St Nicholas Priory played an important role in the religious and social life of Exeter.

Although the church and cloisters were demolished, the remaining buildings and precinct were turned into an impressive Elizabethan town house. After many vicissitudes, the Priory was bought by Exeter Corporation in 1913.

Total refurbishment and a new presentation completed in 2007, including a slide show, give a vivid idea of how the house looked in Elizabethan times. The parlour, for example, has been decorated with hundreds of period stencils and furnished with tables, chairs, platters and cutlery, all using the methods of five centuries ago. Visitors are free to touch and use the replica artefacts. Children are especially fascinated with playing Tudor games and dressing in the costumes provided.

Number 21 The Mint is the Priory's former refectory wing. It too has been sensitively restored and includes many interesting features, including a 15th century arch-braced roof. Both buildings are open to the public at specified times.

Continue down Fore Street for 60 m. Cross Bartholomew Street. (Five metres beyond is RACKCLOSE LANE – see above.) Cross Fore Street and follow WEST STREET downhill, past some interesting Georgian façades, to the 'House that Moved'. On the river side of the House That Moved, a green plaque marks the site of the old West Gate. One of four city gates when Exeter was a walled city, it saw William III's triumphal entry in 1688.

On the landward side, at the foot of Stepcote Hill, are two more timber-framed houses and the church of St Mary Steps. Dating from about 1150, it is famed for its tower clock. Cross WESTERN WAY at the traffic lights. Turn left and 50 m ahead turn right down steps to Cricklepit Mill (page 27).

The St Mary Steps clock, known as 'Matthew the Miller and his Sons', was made in 1619-21. Its quarter jacks, dressed in 17th century costumes, delight children with their chimes

The House that Moved. This 15th century timber-framed merchant's house was jacked up and moved on rollers from its original home in nearby Frog Street in 1961 to prevent its destruction during road widening

Turn left at the Bishop Blaize pub. Take the lane on the left, just beyond the 1681 Custom House (see page 25), easily recognised by its brick façade and the two cannons (1789) in front. (Walk 5 starts from the Quay Interpretation Centre, just ahead of you.)

Turn almost immediately right to follow a section of the city wall uphill. Cross WESTERN WAY by the footbridge. Turn left into SOUTH STREET past the White Hart (page 11). Turn right, PALACE GATE, and return to the Cathedral.

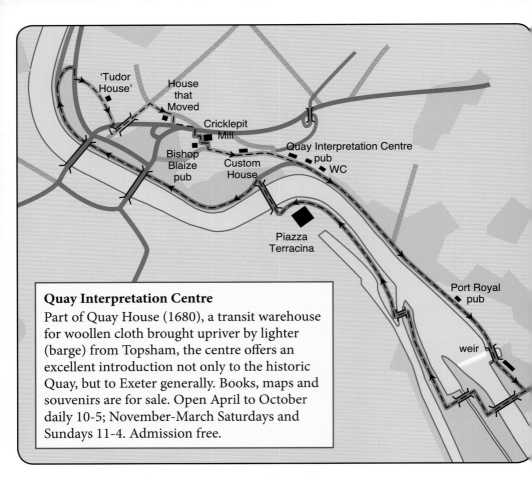

Quay Interpretation Centre

Part of Quay House (1680), a transit warehouse for woollen cloth brought upriver by lighter (barge) from Topsham, the centre offers an excellent introduction not only to the historic Quay, but to Exeter generally. Books, maps and souvenirs are for sale. Open April to October daily 10-5; November-March Saturdays and Sundays 11-4. Admission free.

Walk 5 The Quay, River and Canal

Starting from the Quay Interpretation Centre, this walk can readily be linked to Walk 4.

Facing the Quay Interpretation Centre, turn right and walk past the Prospect Inn. Under the canopy of the transit sheds opposite is the cast iron King's Beam of 1838. Similar to that on Topsham Quay (page 30), it was used to suspend scales for weighing dutiable goods. The tall buildings on the left were warehouses, built during expansion of the Quay in 1835.

From the warehouses, you may shorten your walk by crossing the Exe via the hand-hauled Butts Ferry (seasonal) or take a cruise to the Double Locks. To explore more of the river and canal on foot – a walk of approximately 30 minutes – continue downriver on the footpath,

Top right: The Custom House was built in 1681 when Exeter's cloth trade was booming. It now forms the centre of the newly re-modelled quayside and is Britain's oldest extant customs house; it was in continuous use by HM Customs and Excise until 1989. The exterior is complemented by beautiful plasterwork ceilings inside

Below right: Butts Ferry

but watch out for cyclists. Note the cast-iron lighting standards: they come from the 1905 Exe Bridge, which was replaced by the present utilitarian steel and concrete structures in 1969-72.

Continue downriver past the Port Royal, the weir and the mill buildings (1730). The old millstones have been placed by the path. Turn right ALPHINGTON, crossing the Exe by Trew's Weir suspension bridge. Enjoy the views up and downriver. Cross a second bridge. At this point you might wish to extend your walk by turning left down the EXE CYCLE ROUTE towards the confluence of the canal and river at Turf Hotel (seasonal opening).

Top left: Boats moored in the harbour area

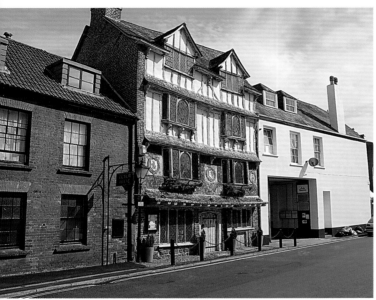

Below left: The four-storey 'Tudor House' which gives its name to Tudor Street is probably misnamed – most authorities now agree it was built in 1660. It has characteristic features from that period, including 'pentices' (the slate slopes), timber framing and locally made brick in the side walls

Otherwise, turn right EXE CYCLE ROUTE CITY CENTRE. Continue upriver, CANAL BASIN AND FERRY, at the next fingerpost. The canal basin was enlarged in 1830 in response to increasing trade and retains period warehouses. Follow the path by the river bank to the modern Piazza Terracina for a good view of the canal basin. On your left as you face the basin is an 1867 railway turntable and a rare example of Brunel's broad gauge track leading from it.

Continue upriver and cross the footbridge, with an excellent view of the Quay. Turn left and walk upriver under the Exe Bridges. Ignore the first flight of steps on the right. Turn right up the concrete ramp ahead and continue to BONHAY ROAD.

Cricklepit Mill is currently open 9-5 Mondays to Fridays, except lunchtimes. Touch screen computers and interpretation boards explain its history, as well as the mechanics of the mill

Cross the road. Turn right and only 20 m ahead turn left into TUDOR STREET. Cross WESTERN WAY with care and climb the steps opposite, up to NEW BRIDGE STREET. There is a good view of the medieval Exe Bridge from here. It was completed in 1238 at a time when the Exe was wider than today and much of the adjoining land was marsh.

Walk left and uphill. Take the first turning right, WEST STREET (for a description of West Street see pages 21-22). Recross WESTERN WAY with care. Turn right, then left into COMMERCIAL ROAD for THE QUAY.

Continue to the Bishop Blaize. The inn is named after the patron saint of cloth workers and houses prints of historic Exeter maps. It is said to date from medieval times and is situated within what was Exeter's industrial heart when the city's wealth was based on woollen cloth processed in water-driven mills. Turn left to Cricklepit Mill to discover more about Exeter's woollen industry.

After visiting Cricklepit Mill, return to the Bishop Blaize and turn left back to the start.

Cricklepit Mill

Cricklepit is the last of nine mills on Exe Island, for centuries Exeter's industrial centre, processing cloth and grinding corn. All the mills were powered by water diverted from the Exe via leats. Restored by Devon Historic Buildings Trust in 2002, Cricklepit is now the headquarters of Devon Wildlife Trust. The mill machinery is in working order for the first time since closure as a commercial mill in the 1970s and Cricklepit grinds corn on special occasions.

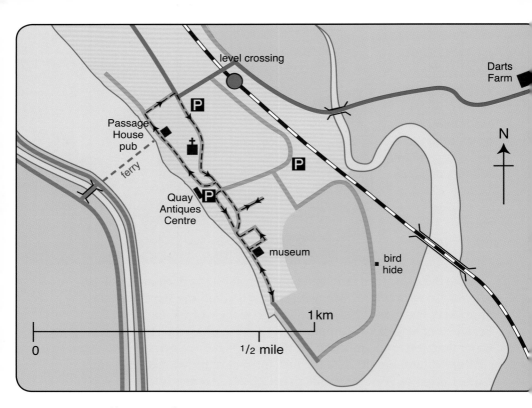

Walk 6 Topsham

Although officially part of Exeter since 1966, Topsham has its own distinctive charm and character. Saved from through traffic and modern developments by its narrow streets, it retains a wealth of historic buildings, mainly from 1660-1730, the period of its greatest prosperity.

Topsham began as a Roman settlement and developed as a Saxon township. It gained its charter in 1257 from Henry III and developed as a wealthy port. Following the construction of Countess Wear (weir) in 1284 and its extension in 1311, ships were unable to reach Exeter's quays and were thus obliged to use Topsham's instead. Although a ship canal opened up to Exeter in 1563, Topsham's trade thrived, especially with the Netherlands and North America.

From the central car park, turn left into Fore Street (or use alternative parking in Holman Way or on the Quay if this is full). Take time to study the Fore Street buildings, many of which are attractive individual shops. For example, number 88 is a pretty brick-fronted Georgian house. The Salutation is a classic coaching inn.

Top right: The Salutation Inn in Fore Street is a classic coaching inn with a splendid Georgian façade, though its core may well be older. The inn's entrance porch projects over the pavement and huge doors lead to the former stables

Below right: The Shell House in The Strand, so named after its shell doorway

Numbers 61 and 62 Fore Street are medieval and number 63 is an altered timber-framed jettied house of the 16th or 17th centuries. The church's red sandstone tower is medieval too, and the font, with its zigzag pattern and animal motif, is Norman.

Continue to the Globe Hotel. The exterior is Georgian, but its lateral chimney stacks, its long, low proportions and the remains of a screens passage inside suggest it is much older. Follow Fore Street as far as the Lighter Inn. Named after the barges that carried goods on to Exeter, the inn is decorated with seascapes and photographs, both contemporary and period. Some show salmon netting on the Exe.

On the Quay is the cast iron 'King's Beam', formerly used to weigh dutiable goods. (There is a similar beam on Exeter Quay, see page 24.) Nearby is Furlong, a two-storey limestone house, once a sail loft.

Continue into the Strand, passing the attractive Shell House of 1571, so named because of its shell porch. Number 25 is one of the Strand's late 17th century merchants' houses and is now Topsham Museum. It is worth visiting for the period furniture and fittings alone, especially the long case clocks and four poster bed, but it also has a fascinating local history collection centred upon maritime trade and shipbuilding. There are boats on display, including the *Cygnet*, built in 1861 in the shape of a swan, a River Exe boat and a skiff, plus special exhibitions of wildlife on the estuary and a room devoted to Vivien Leigh memorabilia.

Continue down the Strand with its gable-fronted Dutch-style houses to the Goat Walk, where there are excellent views of the river. Topsham ships trading with the Netherlands brought back Dutch building styles and small Dutch bricks as their ballast to create one of Devon's most unusual and attractive streets.

At low tide, large flocks of waders and other wildfowl find rich feeding on the mudflats. Huge numbers of migratory birds such as Brent geese can be seen from the Goat Walk in winter. As the tide rises, many birds fly on to Bowling Green Marshes, where there is a convenient bird hide. To reach it, follow the Goat Walk and turn left at Bowling Green Road. After visiting the hide, retrace your steps.

Stroll back along the Strand past the Museum and immediately turn right to explore Lower Shapter Street. Near the end of this street take the alley left into Higher Shapter Street, which again has many interesting Georgian fronts.

Return to the Strand and take the next right up Monmouth Hill (by the Shell House), then turn right again into Monmouth Street, with its imposing houses. Note particularly numbers 36 to 39, built in 1715 with a pair of splendid doorcases and Tuscan columns. Number 29 has end stacks of the characteristic Dutch brick, whilst number 33 has a fine doorcase and a Sun Insurance fire mark.

Retrace your steps down Monmouth Street. Turn right along Monmouth Hill. At the end of Monmouth Hill, turn left just beyond the Lighter Inn. Turn right and follow Ferry Road parallel to the river. Ferry Road has many historic houses with maritime connections, including the 17th century Harbourmaster's House, once the Custom House.

Cruises on the Exe to Turf Lock and Exmouth are offered at Trout's Boatyard, where generations of Trouts have made their living. Further up Ferry Road is the small foot ferry, which offers a short trip across the Exe. On the opposite bank, the path can be followed up river to Exeter or down river to Powderham, seat of the Earls of Devon and open to the public. Beside the ferry is the aptly named Passage House Inn. Continue along Ferry Road. Reaching Follett Road, turn right and right again into Fore Street. Continue to the car park.

Useful information

Details correct at the time of writing, but subject to change.

Exeter Visitor Information & Tickets, Dix's Field:
01392 665700   www.exeter.gov.uk/visiting
Open 9-5 Monday-Saturday, 10-4 Sundays and bank holidays.
Good range of books and maps. This is the best starting point for enquiries. Check for special events, including living history and heritage days.

Cathedral: www.exeter-cathedral.org.uk 01392 255573. Entrance fee for general visitors (except Sundays).

Guildhall: free entry but sometimes closed for business. Check opening times and dates on 01392 665500 www.exeter.gov.uk

Internet: offers a plethora of information.
Try www.exeter.gov.uk/timetrail, www.exetermemories.co.uk

Quay House Visitor Centre: free entry. Audio-visual presentation, displays, illustrations and artefacts.
April to October daily 10-5, November to March weekends 11-4.

Red Coat Tours: free daily guided tours of the city, complementing this book. Booking not required. Operating all year. They start opposite the Royal Clarence (Abode) in Cathedral Green or from Quay House Visitor Centre at 11am and 2pm. Details 01392 265203 www.exeter.gov.uk/guidedtours

Royal Albert Memorial Museum: closed for redevelopment until spring 2010, but its work continues with exhibitions around the city. 01392 665858 www.exeter.gov.uk/ramm

St Nicholas Priory: open to the general public during school holidays Monday to Saturday 10-5, except Bank Holidays; only on Saturdays in term. Entrance fee. 01392 665858 www.exeter.gov.uk

Topsham Museum: 25 The Strand 01392 873244; open April-Oct, Mondays, Wednesdays, Saturdays, and Sundays 2-5. Donations.

Tuckers' Hall: free entry 10.30-12.30 Tuesdays and Thursdays between June and September; Thursday mornings only in winter.

Underground Passages: open daily June to September and school holidays. October to May closed Mondays. Entrance fee.
01392 665887   www.exeter.gov.uk